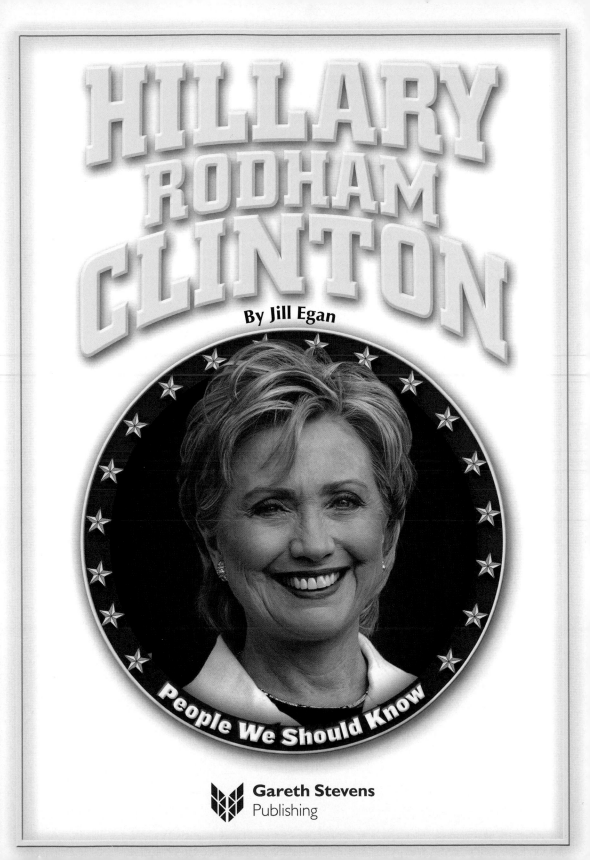

HILLARY RODHAM CLINTON

By Jill Egan

People We Should Know

Gareth Stevens
Publishing

Please visit our web site at **www.garethstevens.com.**
For a free color catalog describing our list of high-quality books,
call 1-800-542-2595 (USA) or 1-800-387-3178 (Canada). Our fax: 1-877-542-2596

Library of Congress Cataloging-in-Publication Data
Egan, Jill.
    Hillary Rodham Clinton / by Jill Egan.
      p. cm. — (People we should know)
    Includes bibliographical references and index.
    ISBN-10: 1-4339-2188-X   ISBN-13: 978-1-4339-2188-9 (lib. bdg.)
    ISBN-10: 1-4339-2193-6   ISBN-13: 978-1-4339-2193-3 (soft cover)
    1. Clinton, Hillary Rodham—Juvenile literature. 2. Presidents' spouses—United States—
    Biography—Juvenile literature. 3. Women legislators—United States—Biography—Juvenile
    literature. 4. United States. Congress. Senate—Biography—Juvenile literature. 5. Women
    presidential candidates—United States—Biography—Juvenile literature. 6. Women cabinet
    officers—United States—Biography—Juvenile literature. I. Title.
  E887.C55E34 2010
  973.929092—dc22 [B]   2009007168

This edition first published in 2010 by
Gareth Stevens Publishing
A Weekly Reader® Company
1 Reader's Digest Road
Pleasantville, NY 10570-7000 USA

Copyright © 2010 by Gareth Stevens, Inc.
Executive Managing Editor: Lisa M. Herrington
Senior Editor: Brian Fitzgerald
Senior Designer: Keith Plechaty

Produced by Editorial Directions, Inc.

Art Direction and Page Production: Kathleen Petelinsek, The Design Lab

Picture credits
Cover and title page: Steve Pope/epa/Corbis; p. 5: Andrew Lichtenstein/Sygma/Corbis; p. 7:
Ray Stubbebine/Getty Images; p. 8: Reuters/Corbis; p. 9: Tim Sloan/AFP/Getty Images; p. 11:
Yearbook Library; p. 13: Bettmann/Corbis; p. 14: Yearbook Library; p. 15: Associated Press;
p. 16: Associated Press; p. 17: NASA; p. 19: Sygma/Corbis; p. 21: Sygma/Corbis; p. 22 Wally
McNamee/Corbis; p. 23: Sygma/Corbis; p. 25: AP Photo; p. 27: The Print Collector/Alamy;
p. 28: Danny Johnston/ Associated Press; p. 29: Reuters/Corbis; p. 31: Schwarz Shaul/Corbis
Sygma; p. 32: Underwood and Underwood/Time & Life/Getty Images; p. 33: Dusan Vranica/
AFP/Getty Images; p. 35: AP Photo/Charlie Neibergall; p. 77: Ronald Karpilo/Alamy; p. 38: Ron
Sachs-Pool/Getty Images; p. 39: Brian Snyder/Reuters/Corbis; p. 41: AP Photo/Elise Amendola;
p. 42: Michael Reynolds/epa/Corbis; p. 43 AP Photo/Manuel Balce Ceneta

Printed in the United States of America

1 2 3 4 5 6 7 8 9 14 13 12 11 10 09

TABLE OF CONTENTS

Words in the glossary appear in **bold** type
the first time they are used in the text.

CHAPTER 1

Candidate Clinton

On the morning of July 7, 1999, **First Lady** Hillary Clinton was about to make history. She announced that she was running to represent New York in the U.S. **Senate**. It was the first time a first lady had ever run for public office.

Many people had wondered if she would someday run for public office. She had spent her entire life fighting for issues she believed in. She cared most about the rights of children and women.

Hillary Clinton speaks with reporters the day she announced her Senate run.

Finally the Candidate

One of New York's two senators, Daniel Patrick Moynihan, was retiring. The United States has two major political parties: the Democrats and the Republicans. Moynihan was a popular Democrat. Many people thought Hillary Clinton would be the best choice to replace him. She had always supported her husband, President Bill Clinton, when he ran for political office. Now she wanted to be the politician.

Fast Fact

The first time Hillary Clinton won an election was in sixth grade. She was voted cocaptain of her school's safety patrol.

The Journey Begins

After leaving the White House, the Clintons had moved to New York state. Hillary Clinton loved the state and knew she wanted to represent it.

As she stepped out to make her announcement, she was surprised at what she saw. As first lady, she was used to seeing reporters. That day, however, more than 200 reporters were there. They all wanted to hear what she had to say.

Clinton took a deep breath and said, "I intend to be spending my time in the next days and weeks and months listening to New Yorkers." Then she said what everyone had waited to hear. Clinton said she wanted to be one of New York's two senators.

"If we work together, we really can make a difference for the children and families in New York."

–Hillary Clinton, to a group of New York teachers

Democrats Choose Their Candidate

When Daniel Patrick Moynihan announced he was retiring from the Senate, the Democratic Party went into action. They wanted the Democrat who ran for Moynihan's seat to be someone voters knew. They decided America's first lady was the best choice. Democrats in New York and across the country urged Hillary Clinton to be their **candidate**.

Clinton meets with Moynihan on his farm near Oneonta, New York. They discussed her Senate plans.

A Listening Tour

Clinton said she was going on a "listening tour" of the state. She said that the issues that were important to New Yorkers were important to her, too. She wanted to travel across the state and hear New Yorkers' opinions. She wanted to meet dairy farmers in rural parts of the state. She also wanted to meet New York City's teachers. She was going to listen to their ideas and concerns.

A group of union members show their support for Clinton in 2000.

Meeting Voters

The Senate election was more than a year away. Clinton wasn't going to waste any time. The same afternoon she made her announcement, she went out to meet with voters.

A **campaign** can be long and difficult, but Clinton enjoyed the experience. She had an easy time connecting with voters. Over the next several months, she met with thousands of people. She said if voters chose her, she would do everything she could to make sure New Yorkers and all Americans were safe and healthy.

Fast Fact

Clinton upset New York Mets baseball fans when she wore a New York Yankees cap during her Senate campaign.

Senator Clinton

The voters liked what she had to say. On November 7, 2000, Hillary Clinton was elected as one of the two U.S. senators from New York. She was the first woman to represent New York in the Senate. She was also the first former first lady to be elected to public office. People around the country watched as Clinton began a new chapter in her life.

On the Campaign Trail

Former president Bill Clinton joins his wife on the campaign trail.

As she was campaigning, Clinton had the chance to try many new foods and activities. She tried salsa dancing, learned how to polka, and ate sausage sandwiches. She visited state fairs, barbecues, and bake sales. After months of travel, she had visited each of New York's 62 counties and met thousands of voters.

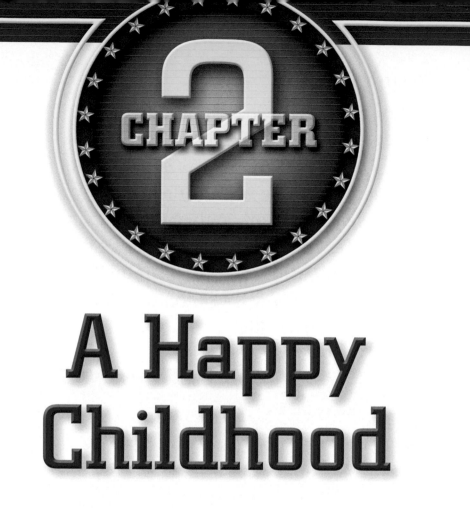

CHAPTER 2

A Happy Childhood

Hillary Diane Rodham was born on October 26, 1947, in Chicago, Illinois. She was the first child of Hugh and Dorothy Rodham. Then came brothers Hugh Jr. and Tony. When Hillary was three years old, the family moved to a suburb called Park Ridge.

It was important to Hillary's parents that their children were healthy and happy. Her father encouraged Hillary to think about politics. Hillary's mother was kind and calm. She told her daughter that she could be anything she wanted.

Hillary (center) poses for a photo while a freshman in high school.

A Regular Girl

At school, Hillary worked hard and earned good grades. When she was young, she had trouble in math. Her father woke up early to help her with her math homework.

Her father also taught her how to play baseball and football. She was considered a tomboy. Her favorite teams were the Chicago Cubs and the New York Yankees. "My parents gave me my belief in working hard," she remembers, "and not being limited by the fact that I was a little girl."

Fast Fact

When she was young, Hillary wore fashionable white gloves when dressing up for special occasions.

Meeting a Civil Rights Hero

When Hillary was in high school, she became more active in social and political activities. She organized a neighborhood carnival and helped register people to vote. She was active in her Girl Scout troop and was a member of her school's student government.

In 1961, when Hillary was 14, she met the Reverend Don Jones. He was the youth minister at the church she attended. In the spring of 1962, **civil rights** leader Martin Luther King Jr. came to speak in Chicago. Jones took Hillary and other youth group members to hear King speak. That was a day Hillary would never forget.

"I was deeply moved then, as I continue to be, by his timeless call to all of us, his dream for a world that is really worthy of our children."

–Hillary Clinton, on Martin Luther King Jr.'s spring 1962 speech

A Civil Rights Leader

Martin Luther King Jr. (1929–1968) is one of the most admired leaders of the civil rights movement. King believed that all people—black and white, poor and rich—should have the same rights. In 1963, he helped organize the March on Washington. It drew nearly 250,000 people to the nation's capital. King moved the nation when he delivered his famous "I have a dream" speech.

Martin Luther King Jr. waves to the crowd during the March on Washington in 1963.

King's Inspiring Words

King talked about racial **segregation**. He explained that African American children didn't have the same rights and opportunities as white children, just because of their skin color. King said that to make sure everyone was treated equally, all people needed to speak out.

The speech inspired Hillary. It was the first time she was aware of the unfairness some people faced. At school and at home, Hillary started to speak out about the **inequalities** she saw.

Standing Strong

As Hillary got older, she saw the **discrimination** that many girls and women experienced. Some of her friends pretended they weren't smart, just to impress boys. Hillary thought this was silly. She knew she was just as smart as any boy.

Hillary (front) was a member of the Honor Society in high school.

A Woman of Firsts

Born in Maine in 1897, Margaret Chase Smith was the first woman elected to both the U.S. **House of Representatives** and the U.S. Senate. She served four terms in each. She was the first woman to enter the Senate without being appointed to the position. She was also the first woman to be nominated for president by a major party. She left the Senate in 1973. She traveled the country giving speeches at colleges. Smith died in 1995.

An Early Hero

In the 1960s, there weren't many women who were leaders in the country. One of Hillary's heroes was Margaret Chase Smith. Smith was a Republican senator from Maine. She was the first woman to run for president for a major party.

Fast Fact

One of Hillary's favorite books was the novel *Little Women*, by Louisa May Alcott.

Running For Office

During her senior year at Park Ridge's Maine South High School, Hillary ran for student government president. She was the only girl who ran. Her opponents were several boys. She lost the election by many votes. One of her opponents told her she was really stupid if she thought a girl could be elected president. The boy's words stung Hillary.

Hillary sits for her senior class photo in 1965.

In 1983, Sally Ride became the first American woman in space.

No Girls Allowed

When she was 14 years old, Hillary thought she wanted to be an astronaut. She wrote a letter to the National Aeronautics and Space Administration (NASA) asking how to become an astronaut. She received a letter back telling her that girls could not be astronauts. In 1978, NASA began accepting women. As of 2009, there are 36 women astronauts in the United States.

Most Likely to Succeed

Although Hillary was hurt by her opponent's comment, she didn't stay down for long. She continued to be herself. As she prepared to graduate in 1965, she was voted "Most Likely to Succeed" in her class. It was clear that Hillary's classmates expected great things from her in the future.

CHAPTER 3

Fighting For Others

In the fall of 1965, Hillary Rodham enrolled in Wellesley College, an all-women's school. She chose to study political science. At first, she was lonely. She struggled to keep up in classes. Before long, things got better.

Rodham was elected president of the Young Republicans club. Soon she realized she was not a young Republican after all. She found that her beliefs were more like those of the Democratic Party. So she became a Democrat.

Hillary Rodham spent four years at Wellesley College.

A Voice For a Generation

In 1969, Hillary Rodham was asked to speak at her graduation ceremony. She was the first student to ever speak at a Wellesley graduation. In her speech, she talked about equal rights and the importance of trust and respect. Some people said she was the voice of her generation. Reporters from across the country wanted to talk to her.

Fast Fact

In 1969, *Life* magazine named Hillary Rodham one of the nation's student leaders. It said she was a symbol of the values of her generation.

Learning About Law

Of the 235 students to enter Yale Law School in the fall of 1969, only 27 were women. Hillary Rodham was one of them. At the time, not many women were lawyers. Some people thought women couldn't be good lawyers. Rodham wanted to prove those people wrong.

At law school, she focused on working for children's rights. "I realized that what I wanted to do with the law was to give voice to children who were not being heard," she said. She met Marian Wright Edelman, who became her adviser. Edelman had founded the Children's Defense Fund, an organization that helps poor and **minority** children. Rodham went to work for the organization.

Fast Fact

Hillary Rodham spent the summer before law school working at a fish cannery in Alaska.

"The challenge now is to practice politics as the art of making what appears to be impossible, possible."

–Hillary Rodham to her graduating class in 1969

Bill Clinton and Hillary Rodham began dating while they were both at Yale.

Bill Clinton

William Jefferson "Bill" Clinton loved politics from a young age, though his first career goal was to be a jazz saxophonist. He served as U.S. president from 1993 to 2001. When Hillary Rodham Clinton ran for the U.S. Senate, Bill campaigned for her harder than anyone.

Meeting Bill Clinton

In 1971, Hillary Rodham met the man who would change her life. Bill Clinton was a tall, friendly, and outspoken law student from Arkansas. Hillary and Bill talked about politics, family, and their goals. Soon they fell in love.

When they finished law school in 1973, Hillary continued to work for the Children's Defense Fund. She loved her job. Bill asked Hillary several times to marry him, but she wasn't ready.

Moving to Arkansas

Hillary Rodham was quickly making a name for herself as a lawyer. She was asked to work on a committee that was investigating President Richard Nixon. There were 44 lawyers on the committee, and only three were women. Some of the committee's work led Nixon to resign, or quit, the presidency in 1974.

Around this time, Bill decided to move back to Arkansas. He wanted to make a difference in his home state. He wanted to be governor. Hillary decided to go with him. They were married on October 11, 1975.

Hillary Rodham discusses the Nixon investigation with fellow lawyers.

What's in a Name?

After she married, Hillary decided to keep Rodham as her last name. Arkansas voters didn't like that. They thought the first lady should have her husband's last name. When Bill lost a reelection campaign, people said it was Hillary's fault. In 1982, he ran again. She changed her name to Hillary Rodham Clinton to help Bill get reelected.

Finding Success

Hillary Rodham had developed a reputation as a talented lawyer. In 1975, she became a professor at the University of Arkansas School of Law. A few years later, she became the first female lawyer at the largest law firm in Arkansas.

In 1978, Bill Clinton was elected governor of Arkansas, and Hillary Rodham would be the state's first lady. As first lady, she could help improve people's lives. She fought for children's rights and worked to improve public education in Arkansas. Bill and Hillary were busy at work and at home. In 1980, their daughter, Chelsea, was born.

Fast Fact

Chelsea was named for her parents' favorite song, "Chelsea Morning," which was sung by Judy Collins.

CHAPTER 4

America's First Lady

By 1991, Bill Clinton was in his fifth term as governor of Arkansas. That year, he announced his plan to run for president of the United States. Hillary was his biggest supporter. Bill and Hillary told the American people that together, they could do twice as much work for the American people. Bill said voters could "buy one, get one free."

Hillary worked hard to make sure Bill was elected. She traveled across the country, speaking to people about issues that she and Bill cared about.

Hillary Clinton worked very closely with her husband, Bill, during his campaign for president.

A Tough Campaign

Voters were curious about Hillary. All the attention was difficult sometimes. It was hard to hear people say that she wouldn't be a good first lady or that Bill wouldn't be a good president. She reminded herself that politics isn't easy.

Hillary helped convince Americans Bill should be president. On November 3, 1992, voters elected Bill Clinton. Hillary would be America's new first lady.

Fast Fact

Hillary Rodham Clinton read a biography on each of the previous 42 first ladies before her husband became president.

Working For Better Health Care

Hillary Rodham Clinton was excited to be the country's first lady. She wanted to take part in changing policy. President Clinton put her in charge of a team whose goal was to make health care better. That meant finding ways to help make doctor and hospital visits affordable.

The Clintons believed everyone had a right to good health care. Hillary Rodham Clinton was the first first lady to create government policy and to introduce proposed laws to Congress. She worked hard to get a new health care law passed.

> **"**We are so fortunate to have a first lady who has fought for and will continue to fight for the rights of children.**"**
>
> –Performer Barbra Streisand, after Bill Clinton's election

Eleanor Roosevelt, Role Model

Hillary Clinton has said that reading about her role model, Eleanor Roosevelt (who died in 1962), helped her get through hard times. Eleanor was married to Franklin D. Roosevelt, who was president from 1933 to 1945. The two first ladies had a lot in common. Like Clinton, Roosevelt was an outspoken woman who worked for causes she believed in, even if they weren't popular.

When Roosevelt was first lady, many people said she should keep her ideas to herself. She refused. Roosevelt's example helped Hillary Clinton to continue speaking out about her beliefs.

Health Care Plan Defeated

Many people opposed the health care plan. Some criticized Clinton, saying that a first lady should not be working to change policy. Getting the lawmakers in Congress to vote the plan into law became difficult. After all her work, Congress never voted on the plan. News reporters said the plan was a failure. Hillary Rodham Clinton had to find another way to improve people's lives.

Still in the Fight

Hillary Clinton continued to work to help people. As first lady, she traveled to more than 80 countries. She met with leaders to discuss ways to improve rights for women and children. She encouraged all women to speak their minds.

In 1996, Bill won a second term as president. Hillary continued fighting to improve people's rights. She hosted many conferences on women's and children's issues. That same year, she wrote a book called *It Takes a Village and Other Lessons Children Teach Us*. It became a best seller.

Hillary Rodham Clinton speaks to a crowd on her book tour for *It Takes a Village* in 1996.

Meet the First Pets

When the Clintons went to the White House, they brought their black-and-white cat, Socks. In 1997, Socks got an unwelcome roommate. The Clintons adopted an energetic chocolate Labrador named Buddy. Socks and Buddy did not get along. Kids across the country wrote letters to the pets. In 1998, Hillary put together a book of the letters titled *Dear Socks, Dear Buddy: Kids' Letters to the First Pets.*

Buddy, the first dog, walks with the Clintons.

The End of the White House Years

The end of the Clintons' time in the White House was not easy. Chelsea left for Stanford University in California. President Clinton faced a tough fight to keep his job after he was **impeached**. Throughout these challenges, Hillary Clinton was determined to keep working. She remembered what her pastor had told her when she was young. He said, when you are down, do something to help others to lift you back up.

CHAPTER 5

Senator Clinton

In 1999, the Clintons started to think about life after the White House. They looked for a new place to live. They settled on Chappaqua, New York.

Later that year, Hillary decided to run for the U.S. Senate. She wanted to represent her new home state. After months of campaigning, Election Day arrived. On November 7, 2000, Bill and Chelsea joined Hillary as she went to vote. "After seeing Bill's name on ballots for years, I was thrilled and honored to see my own," she said.

Hillary Rodham Clinton campaigns
for a Senate seat in 2000.

Election Night

On Election Night, the results came in
quickly. It was clear who the winner was.
Chelsea delivered the news to her mom.
Clinton beat her Republican opponent,
55 percent to 43 percent.

That night, she spoke before cheering
supporters. Confetti and balloons filled
the air as Clinton hugged her family and
friends. She was now Senator Clinton
from New York.

Fast Fact

In 2000, Chelsea
took off a
semester from
college to help
her mother
campaign for the
Senate seat.

Women in the Senate

Only 38 women have served in the U.S. Senate since the 100-member group first met in 1789. The first elected female senator was Hattie Carraway of Arkansas. She served from 1932 to 1945. In the late 2000s, there were 17 women serving as senators. When Hillary Clinton became secretary of state in 2009, a woman, Kirsten Gillibrand, replaced her in the Senate.

Hattie Carraway was the first elected female member of the Senate.

Life in the Senate

As a new senator, Hillary Clinton received a lot of attention. People wondered if the former first lady would do a good job in her new role. Clinton's ability was tested early on.

On September 11, 2001, terrorist attacks took place in New York City, Pennsylvania, and Washington, D.C. It was a tragic day. Clinton was able to get Congress to approve emergency money and services for the people of New York City. She helped the city recover.

A Tough Job

In 2002, senators were asked to vote on President George W. Bush's request to go to war in Iraq. Senator Clinton and most other senators voted yes. The U.S. went to war in 2003. During the war, Clinton visited troops in Iraq.

Soon Clinton decided the war was not going in the right direction. She wanted the U.S. military to leave Iraq. She began to speak out about her views. People across the country listened. They wanted to hear more from Senator Clinton.

Fast Fact

Clinton's memoir, *Living History*, was a best seller when it was published in 2003.

Senator Clinton visits U.S. troops in Baghdad, Iraq, in 2003.

Working With Many People

Senator Clinton served on many important committees. She developed a reputation for working with Democrats and Republicans. She remained interested in issues that affect families and children.

Before long, Clinton was selected as a member of the powerful Armed Services Committee. This committee talks about issues involving the U.S. military. This was a big deal for a first-term senator. General John Keane, then a high-ranking official in the U.S. Army, met with Clinton. "She had an extraordinary grasp of our military culture," he said.

❝I will do everything I can to ensure the same choices, opportunities, and dreams for all of America's children, now and for the future.❞

–Hillary Clinton, in a campaign speech to New Yorkers

Chelsea Clinton

When Chelsea lived in the White House, the Secret Service gave her a fitting nickname: Energy. Chelsea is known for always being on the go and never getting tired. In 2003, Chelsea moved to New York City, where she works in business. She says her most important job has been supporting her mother's political campaigns.

Chelsea Clinton (right) has supported her mother's political ambitions.

A Second Term in the Senate

In 2006, Clinton was up for reelection. This time, she won with 67 percent of the vote. A majority of New Yorkers thought Senator Clinton was doing a great job in politics. She was winning admirers across the country, too.

As she entered her second term, people asked Clinton if she had thought of running for president. Many people told Clinton that she was the person they wanted in the White House. She started to think being president was a job she might want.

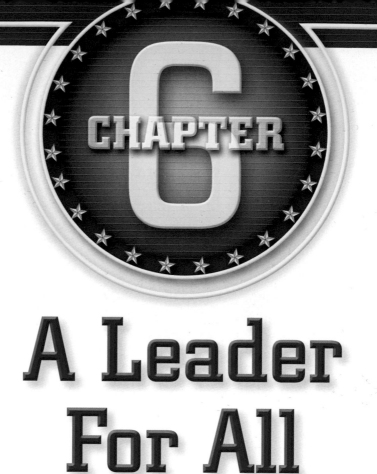

CHAPTER 6

A Leader For All

On January 20, 2007, Senator Hillary Clinton posted a message on her web site: "I'm in. And I'm in to win." She had just announced she was running for president of the United States.

Several women had run for the nation's highest office. Clinton's childhood hero, Margaret Chase Smith, had tried for the Republican nomination in 1964. In 1972, Shirley Chisholm had tried to win the nomination of the Democratic Party. Neither of these women had been successful.

Clinton speaks to a large crowd during her campaign for president.

"I Think I Can Win"

Clinton said she wanted to run for president to improve health care and public education. She said improving the economy was especially important. Republican George W. Bush was the nation's president at the time. She and other Democrats were disappointed with many Republican policies. "I'm running because I think I can win and I can take the White House back," Clinton said.

Fast Fact

Clinton was one of the first candidates to use the Internet to connect with voters. She set up a web site, a blog, and MySpace and Facebook pages to help her reach voters.

Barack Obama

Barack Obama first caught the nation's attention when he gave a speech at the 2004 Democratic **National Convention**. His message of hope and change inspired many people. Famous people, including Oprah Winfrey, Colin Powell, and even Bill Clinton's vice president, Al Gore, supported Obama. Obama made history when he became the nation's first African American president in 2009.

A Historic Race

The race for the Democratic nomination was long and difficult. Many of the candidates were Hillary Clinton's friends and fellow senators. Her main rival was Illinois senator Barack Obama.

Voters were excited. If Clinton won the nomination, she had a good chance of becoming the first female president in U.S. history. If Obama won, he had a good chance of becoming the country's first African American president. People sensed that history was about to be made.

A Close Race

In early 2008, Clinton won a series of **party primaries**. These are state elections that help decide who a party's candidate will be. When she won the New Hampshire primary, her supporters were excited. Many believe that whoever wins in New Hampshire will win the party's nomination. Obama came in a close second.

One by one, the other Democratic candidates dropped out of the race. Soon just Clinton and Obama remained. The campaign polls and primary election results showed the two candidates were almost tied.

Clinton celebrates after her victory in the New Hampshire primary.

Ending the Campaign

As the campaign went on, Obama won more support. Eventually, there was no way Clinton could catch up to Obama.

On June 7, 2008, Clinton announced the end of her campaign. She promised to keep fighting, however. "I've had every opportunity and blessing in my own life, and I want the same for all Americans. And until that day comes, you'll always find me on the front lines of **democracy**, fighting for the future," she said.

Obama acknowledged Clinton's historic run for the presidency. He said, "Because of what Hillary has accomplished, my daughters and yours [are] dreaming a little bigger and setting their sights a little higher today."

Not Quite There

As a presidential candidate, Clinton earned more votes than any woman in U.S. history. Still, many people believe that she experienced different treatment because she is a woman. The press and political experts discussed her hair and clothes. They even made fun of her laugh. Clinton shrugged off the criticism. She said the issues were what people should focus on.

Hillary Clinton campaigns for Barack Obama in 2008.

Supporting Obama

Clinton was sad that her campaign was over. However, she said it was important to keep working to change America. She said she would vote for Obama. She asked others to do the same. At the Democratic National Convention in August 2008, Clinton spoke to the crowd. "Barack Obama is my candidate," she said. "And he must be our president."

Obama ran against Republican nominee John McCain. Clinton worked hard to get her former rival elected. With her help, Obama won the election on November 4, 2008.

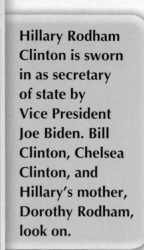

Hillary Rodham Clinton is sworn in as secretary of state by Vice President Joe Biden. Bill Clinton, Chelsea Clinton, and Hillary's mother, Dorothy Rodham, look on.

A New Role

Soon after Obama was elected president, he nominated Clinton to be his secretary of state. She accepted. The job is the most important in the president's cabinet, or group of advisers. The secretary of state makes sure the United States has good relationships with foreign countries. Obama said that Clinton "possesses an extraordinary intelligence and a remarkable work ethic."

On January 21, 2009, Hillary Clinton became the secretary of state. She is the first former first lady to have a position in a president's cabinet. She is the third woman to serve as secretary of state.

Fast Fact

When Hillary Clinton took the oath as secretary of state, she placed her hand on her father's Bible.

Madam Secretary

In 1997, Madeleine Albright was sworn in as the first female secretary of state, under President Bill Clinton. In 2005, President George W. Bush appointed another woman, Condoleezza Rice, to the position. The two women shared another connection. Albright's father, Josef Korbel, was a mentor to Rice when he was her professor at the University of Denver.

Condoleeza Rice served as secretary of state from 2005 to 2009.

Secretary of State Clinton

By becoming secretary of state, Clinton had worked her way to one of the most powerful jobs in the country. In that role, she may be the most powerful woman in the world. Along the way, the young girl from Illinois has become a historic figure. She has helped improve people's rights, education, and health care. Hillary Rodham Clinton has lived a life of firsts. Her first priority, though, has always been to help others live a better life.

Time Line

1947	Hillary Diane Rodham is born on October 26 in Chicago, Illinois.
1969	Hillary Rodham earns a degree in political science from Wellesley College.
1973	Hillary Rodham earns a law degree from Yale University.
1975	Hillary Rodham marries Bill Clinton. Daughter Chelsea is born in 1980.
1979	Hillary Rodham becomes Arkansas's first lady when Bill Clinton is sworn in as governor.
1993	When Bill Clinton takes office as president of the United States, Hillary Rodham Clinton becomes first lady.
2000	Hillary Rodham Clinton wins a seat as a U.S. senator from New York.
2007	Hillary Rodham Clinton declares on January 20 she is a presidential candidate for the Democratic Party.
2009	Hillary Rodham Clinton takes office as secretary of state on January 21.

Glossary

campaign: a race between candidates for an office or position

candidate: a person who is running for office

civil rights: rights of citizens to political and social equality and freedom

democracy: a form of government that is organized and run by the people

discrimination: unfair treatment of one person or a group because of race, age, religion, or gender

first lady: the wife of the president of the United States or of a state's governor

House of Representatives: a house of the U.S. Congress, with 435 voting members elected to two-year terms

impeached: charged with wrongdoing

inequalities: the instances of unfairness or of being unequal

minority: a group of people of a certain race, religion, or background who live among a larger group of a different race, religion, or background. Minority groups in the United States include Hispanic Americans, African Americans, and Asian Americans.

national convention: a large gathering at which a political party officially announces its candidates for president

party primaries: state elections in which members of a political party vote for their candidate for president

segregation: the act of separating groups based on race, gender, or ethnic group

Senate: a house in the U.S. Congress, with 100 voting members elected to six-year terms

Find Out More

Books

Clinton, Hillary Rodham. *Dear Socks, Dear Buddy: Kids' Letters to the First Pets*. New York: Simon & Schuster, 1998.

Hubbard-Brown, Janet. *Eleanor Roosevelt* (Women of Achievement). New York: Chelsea House Publications, 2009.

Krull, Kathleen. *Hillary Rodham Clinton: Dreams Taking Flight*. New York: Simon & Schuster Books for Young Readers, 2008.

Thimmesh, Catherine. *Madam President: The Extraordinary, True (and Evolving) Story of Women in Politics*. Boston: Houghton Mifflin, 2004.

Web Sites

U.S. Department of State: Meet the Secretary
http://future.state.gov/who/secretary/index.htm
Learn more about the office of secretary of state.

White House 101
http://www.whitehouse.gov/about/white_house_101
Read about the history of the White House and the people (and pets) who have lived there.

Source Notes

p. 6: Adam Nagourney, "Moving to Ease Doubts, First Lady Says She Will Enter Senate Race," *New York Times*, November 24, 1999, New York and Region section.

p. 6: Carl Bernstein, *A Woman in Charge: The Life of Hillary Rodham Clinton* (New York: Vintage Books, 2008), 540.

p. 11: Hillary Rodham Clinton, *Living History* (New York: Scribner, 2003), 11.

p. 12: "Clinton on Anniversary of Martin Luther King Jr.'s Trip to India," America. gov, February 12, 2009, www.america.gov/st/texttrans-english/2009/February/20090213115154eaifas0.2894098.html

p. 20: Clinton, 41.

p. 20: Clinton, 50.

p. 24: Clinton, 105.

p. 26: Bernstein, 230.

p. 30: Clinton, 523.

p. 34: Clinton, 532.

p. 34: Karen Tumulty, "Hillary: Love Her, Hate Her," *Time*, August 20, 2006.

p. 36: Dan Balz, "Hillary Clinton Opens Presidential Bid," *Washington Post*, January 21, 2007, A01.

p. 37: Bernstein, 564.

p. 40: "Obama Talks About Glass Ceilings, Child Care, Equal Pay," CNN.com, July 10, 2008, www.cnn.com/2008/POLITICS/07/10/obama.women/index.html.

p. 40: "Hillary Clinton Endorses Barack Obama" (transcript), *New York Times*, June 7, 2008.

p. 41: "Clinton: Obama 'Must Be Our President,' " CNN, August 27, 2008, http://edition.cnn.com/2008/POLITICS/08/26/dnc.main/index.html.

p. 42: "Obama Names Hillary Clinton, Gates to Cabinet," NPR.org, December 1, 2008, www.npr.org/templates/story/story.php?storyId=97632302.

Index

About the Author

Jill Egan is a freelance writer who has written about the people and events that shape our world. When she's not writing, she enjoys exploring new places—both in person and through the pages of books. Born and raised in Juneau, Alaska, Jill now lives with her husband and two cats in San Francisco, California.